out of the silence
poetry by stanley hockman

©2000 by Stanley Hockman

All rights reserved. No part of this publication may be reproduced, stored in a retrieval system, or transmitted, in any form or by any means, electronic, mechanical, photo-copying, recording, or otherwise, without the written prior permission of the author.

Canadian Cataloguing in Publication Data

Hockman, Stanley.
 Out of the silence

 ISBN 1-55212-423-1

 I. Title.
PR6058.O262O97 2000   821'.92   C00-910810-6

TRAFFORD

This book was published *on-demand* in cooperation with Trafford Publishing.
On-demand publishing is a unique process and service of making a book available for retail sale to the public taking advantage of on-demand manufacturing and Internet marketing.
On-demand publishing includes promotions, retail sales, manufacturing, order fulfilment, accounting and collecting royalties on behalf of the author.

Suite 6E, 2333 Government St., Victoria, B.C. V8T 4P4, CANADA
 Phone   250-383-6864   Toll-free   1-888-232-4444 (Canada & US)
 Fax   250-383-6804   E-mail   sales@trafford.com
 Web site www.trafford.com   TRAFFORD PUBLISHING IS A DIVISION OF TRAFFORD HOLDINGS LTD.
 Trafford Catalogue #00-0088   www.trafford.com/robots00-0088.html

Dedication

*To Neale Donald Walsch,
a messenger of God
and author of the
"Conversations with God"
trilogy.*

*Neale is the prime inspiration
in the continuing
growth of my consciousness.*

Also by Stanley Hockman

"open eye, open heart"
    - haiku and two sagas

Acknowledgements

I am grateful to Michaela Davidson for the cover from her painting "Pacific Breakers". And to Anne Harrison, my editor. Their contributions are significant.

foreword

Haiku illuminate what is happening in this place at this moment. My longer poems are derivatives of the short, concise haiku form. They are direct, immediate exposures of my loves, fears, insights, and are all expressions of my level of consciousness at the time of writing - a level that continues to evolve.

My poetry is an invitation to share wondrous, palpable encounters I have with Nature, with my nature, and with God.

The book is in four parts. The last two are related - **"at odds with God"** *on p 83 and* **"as God and I awaken"** *on p 101.*

contents

in the moment   1
  in the forests on the shores

conceiving the pearl   47
  stories I tell myself

at odds with God   83
  separation

as God and I awaken   101
  at-one-ment

in the moment

in the forests on the shores

drumbeats

out of a distant silence
over the waters
through the mists
drumbeats
of an ancient people

lush of the rainforest

on the trail
awash with rivulets
liquid squelch
     of luscious mud
red ferment
        of rotting cedar
lush of the rainforest
green in my nostrils

beside dripping trees
the lake
    it's mirror
freckled
    by raindrops

scimitar

against the sunset
black mountains

on the rim of the sky
wisp of crescent moon
ghosting through dark clouds

the sun sinks

now
etched yellow into the sky
this vast
    curving
        scimitar

race to nowhere

in the warming sun
crunching sand
    scanning the sea
the wind
hollowing out my ears
I race to nowhere
with an apple
a note book
and the resounding
    presence of me

clouds under my feet

in the long low
    murmurings of the sea
on a long wet beach
I
walking barefoot in the dusk
    scattering clouds
        under my feet

scattering the night

through a seamless
opalescent dome
of sea and sky
the sun
    pierces
scattering the night
and the sea
suddenly molten
ripples blue
    ripples gold
        scintillating sunlight

plunging

*plunging
down
into green darkness
sunlight
in shafts of light*

*plunging
down
into dim pools
waterfalls
in plumes of white*

conversation

*a pleasant hour
passes swiftly by
while I converse
with two grazing geese*

*then off they swim
ruffling
the image
of the great green
Bear Mountain*

lakeside

through the mists
ghost trees

over the water
leaning
flaming madronas

plunging down
shimmering silver
on upturned leaves
the sunlight

reaching out
      across the lake
slow ripples
ruffle
the imaged blue of sky

sudden splashing
of mallard wings
      beating the water

then a long silence
on the stillness of the lake

a bite into my apple
would offend

a sudden rabbit

stillness of the forest
sibilance of waves
wind in my hair
the sea
    to my right
trees to my left
    my path
        nowhere
and everywhere

alone among the trees
my heart dredges sadness

a sudden rabbit!

and joy abounds

greetings

anticipating
sunrise
a little breeze
lifts the leaves
and
in the bay
small waves
rise in greeting

senses full and drowning

nostrils wide
breathing in the fragrance
of tar and flowers
and fresh-caught fish
I lie down
head back
sponging impressions
my senses full
and drowning

from blue heights
sunlight tumbles down
warming my skin

punctuating the quiet
with exclamation points
a boat buzzes by

an old airplane roars
and at the edge of sight
a cavalcade of flags
red
    and blue
        and yellow
splashing vivid
        against the sky

the soft murmur
of one wavelet
falling upon the other

            continues.........

I sit up
see the wet
 tangled tresses
of beached seaweed
green
 bronze
and silky burnt umber

beached logs
carved smooth
 and slick
  and white
naked in the sunlight

and over pale winter waters
plummeting
 blue
  flash

kingfisher fishing

birds from nowhere

*but for one lonely cormorant
this morning
I'm up before the birds*

*shivering
I await the rising sun
but the clouds
are ahead of me*

*come sun
you've hidden
long enough
the birds
and I
await breakfast*

*good morning sun!
warmth at last
my fingers
were getting too cold to write*

*and as I watch
      the rising sun
the sea shimmers into colours
and birds
      appear from nowhere*

midwinter

in soft sibilance
           waves ripple
onto pebble-speckled
icy beaches
where bleached
beached logs
bask in the
    midwinter sun

anticipation

the wintered soil
lies black and hard and bare

in my imagination
I search for flowers
and stark branches festoon
with sudden blossom buds

a breeze seems to
breathe over my skin
and the pale pall of winter
passes
my skin tingling
in antipation
of a warming sun

I just walk

white bottoms up
gone in a flash
ducklings diving
with never a splash

scattering water
in wilding flight
two buffleheads
furious
in mating fight

on a bare winter branch
an eagle
scanning the horizon
with imperial glance

gulls screech
it's breakfast talk
crows squabble
flutter and squawk

me
I just walk

great green slow motion

the long muffled thunder
the sighing
soughing murmur
of waves
unfolding
curling down
in great green
    slow motion

shorebirds

long neck
high in pride
stilt-legged
blue heron
pacing out territory

in electric
quickstep
nervous
sandpipers
peppering the beach

on the shining shoreline
migrant
black brant
in darkling shapes

summer evening

the fragrance of green
moist in my nostrils

under my lids
sunshine
dappling
black and gold

in a vastness of blue
seagulls
washed white in sunlight

and as the evening cools
a gossamer breeze
        a silken sheet
rolls over the park

raku boulders

fired and cured
in the heart of volcanoes
raku boulders
aubergine
    black
rounded
voluptuous
   smooth as breasts

like New Yorkers

wild roses
each so precious
  I wouldn't
    dare pick one

dewdrops
each so fragile
  I wouldn't
    wipe one away

sudden
cacophony
of crowing crows
just like New Yorkers

survival

growing seemingly
from the same root
rearing up into the sunlight
cedar and hemlock
entwined
in a timeless agony
of survival

the day's long dawning

waiting
for the day's long dawning
black against the pale sky
two crows

in royal procession
gliding serene
on their reflections
a flotilla of swans

bigger than his mother
cheeping plaintively
feed me! feed me!
a gull chick

vanishing into
      the rising sun
raucously honking
a gaggle of geese

loving waters

in splashes of dappling sunshine
    water
        flowing
            in liquid light

autumn leaves
   on an emerald pool
      like gilded Spanish galleons
     sails unfurled

caressed
    embraced in loving waters
        boulders
            snug in the river's bed

dusk

on a long
       long shore
slow rumble
of mile-long waves

on hightide lines
smash of shells
scatter of crab legs
shards of seagull feasts

on a darkening sea
flash
of lone lighthouse

busy shoreline

*police-ing the shoreline
back and forth
a flight of canada geese*

*seagulls
winging into the wild wind*

*seals smoothing down
into the deeps*

*among a gaggle
of gobbling geese
a heron
solitary on one foot*

*a lone loon poises
dives
and flies down
deep under water*

spring

*willow
branches
drooping
in
whispers
of
yellow
and
green*

*silent
explosions
of
pink
cherry
blossoms*

hopalong crow

*cold ocean here
no scourge of tourists
and on all the long beaches
only one
        hopalong
  crow*

interloper

on the beach
two geese honking

I honk back

they fly away

a lone dog
stops
looks at me haughtily
barks

chases me away

rocks

ancient
etched darkly
by the blasts of time

rocks

bronze-glazed
in the ceramic heat
      of volcanoes

colours of spring

*etched white against
blue sky
magnolia blooms*

*splashed pink
onto green lawns
cherry blossoms*

scents

*on the wet hard sand
walking jauntily
on my reflection
I stride out*

*blown by the wind
I walk six miles
nostrils wide
eyes keening
until a scented lady jogs by*

evening

waves
translucent
seagreen
curling
into wilding whites
of foam

clutched and thrust
in the long reach
of the sea
pebbles rolling
roiling
grinding into sand

pools enrocked
green
in the silence
of stagnation

long shadows
    pacing out the afternoon
into evening

open-eyed

*walking a mile-long beach
there's just me
open-eyed*

*in slow motion
flapping up
into the wind
long-limbed heron*

*from a soft sandcliff
slow
avalanche of sand*

*in searing sunlight
yellow seaweed
bleaching
parchment white*

*beached logs
in random abandon
fallen totems
sleeping in the sun*

caring not
for tomorrow

the cool
of autumn mountains
soft in ocean mists
the air sweet in my breath

the sun shining on my face
soft sand under my feet

the breakers
thundering in my ears

on the horizon
a single fishing boat
white
      in the vastness of blue

on the low-tide shoreline
tiny waves tumbling
swishing
into a million bursting bubbles

in the green
spreading water
filigree patterns of white foam

on the beach
pebbles
in random symmetry
shining wet
      in the sunlight

continues.......

caring not for tomorrow
I walk
fulfilled
breathing in the sea

sleeping leviathans

biting
into soft sea mists
dragon teeth rocks

waves breaking
gulls flying
beaches wearing down

and from the vast
        ocean deeps
tummy rumbles
of sleeping leviathans

a single dandelion

I climb a thousand feet

on the way I count
seventeen shades of green

crawling to a cliff edge
I peer through
      the wild grass
and there
yellow
against the vast
blue of the Pacific
      a single dandelion

way
   way
below
vast rocks
     whirlpooling
       the waves
into a
    wild whiteness

sudden black bear

sitting on the stump
of a moulding red cedar
I count the fall
    of raindrops

in a grove of spiderwebs
      and sun-dappled leaves
a single bird singing

stranded on the footpath
fat like a beached whale
a slug
  sleek
     black
       shining

of a sudden
          a black bear!

my cheeks quiver with fright

s l o w l y
    I m o v e a w a y

alert to the moment

*alert only
to the moment
sage fishing cormorant*

*perched on a log
mindful seagull*

*long neck
comfortably tucked in
heron
in purposeful flight*

*high in the sky
poised to dive
eagle-eyed eagle*

golden waves

*against the setting sun
in the myriad reflections
     of a vast molten sea
waves undulate in gold
     and scattered islands
darken into silhouette*

abundant waters

*piercing
the
calm
of the abundant waters
circling
    diving
        gorging
seagulls*

night senses

*bark
of lone seal surfacing*

*shriek of gulls
in herring-ball frenzy*

*waves
black and white
plashing
splashing
on dark sands*

*sharp in the night air
smoke of campfire*

*stars white
bright
in velvet night*

sonora desert

*seeming to grasp up
into the hot air
many-fingered cacti
green
in a desert
blazing with flowers*

*in an azure sky
circling
      buzzard*

*in a mountain oasis
hot head
  under
    waterfall*

on the beach

cutting into the blue
white scimitar of sail

feathers white
in fading sunlight
seagulls
in darkening sky

on his back
paws on chest
chomping otter

moulded into iron
poised
long S-curve
of heron

tummies flashing white
wheeling
*   sandpipers*
in flight

cooling her wings
in the soft breeze
far-from-home
snowgoose

scurrying
peeping fiercely
hungry
tiny sandpipers

continues......

*sudden scintillation
of turquoise dragonfly*

*picked clean
on the white sands
bleached bones of dog*

lilac

*before dawn
walking down
the centre
of the street
and every block
or two
the scent of lilac*

and the day goes by

over the waters
gliding sedately
*   wings outspread*
sage-faced pelicans

trailing
* a speeding*
*   fishing boat*
* black birds*
*   shrieking*

on the shore
*   in the desert*
green cacti
blue sky
dry dusty wind

in the setting sun
dark mountains
adamantine
in misted valleys

and the day goes by

glide glide flap flap flap

black
slim
high-flying frigate

circling
in silent predation
eagle

watchful
waiting
perched
buzzard

glide
      glide
flap
flap
flap
      glide
          glide
flap
flap
flap

pelicans gliding

      pelicans flapping

            continues.......

flick
hover
  flick
  hover
    flash!

hummingbirds
hovering

then off they dash

pelicans pelicans

pelicans pelicans
delight
delight
Mexican pelicans
in flip-flapping
flight

pelicans
in
ones
pelicans
in
twos
pelicans
patrolling
wherever
they
choose

high adventure!

*lying on grass
I take root*

cannot move

*emulating
a seal's bark*

I nearly expire

*having moved food
from pack
    to stomach
I walk with
straighter back*

senses swooning

*in the heavy fragrance
of honeysuckle
and wild roses
senses swooning
I plunge into the woods*

on goldstream trail

washing leaves
into myriad greens
yellow sunlight

in depths
of swampwater
splendour of clouds

in dead red cedar
new life abounding

in backlit
sunlit leaves
birdsong
and green silence

at the edge of sight
scintillating
symmetries of spiderwebs

in falling light
pouring plunging
     splashing
waterfall

through treetops
first blooming
of stars

before dawn

*floating on the mists of morning
ghost mountains*

*against a gilded sky
                   silhouettes of seagulls*

*on the beach
    skittering
  twittering
breakfasting sandpipers*

*undulating in moving water
sinuous black reflection
of heron*

goldstream

*long soughing
of windswept trees*

*whitecaps of water
rippling
in fast eddies
scattering sunlight
plunging
in torrents
then resting awhile
reflecting
    in shadowed pools*

lushness

lush
lush is the forest floor
wet
*   wet*
green
*   green*
*   green*

and it's not every day
I get to pee
on a centuries-old tree

red sands

on the red sands
of the Algarve
the uneven fall
*   the roar*
and swish
*   and swash*
of ageless waves

birds at work

*eagle
pauses*

plummets

pounces

poor fish

*fast-flapping
butt-heavy
loon
in
long
    long
        take-off*

*pecking
effortlessly
into
the
falling
tide
guileless
gulls*

warm seas

seemingly
up
into the sky
a yacht sails out
as the sea layers
towards the sky
turquoise
    to indigo
        into opalescence

a warm breeze blows
palms bend
and I drift
    in lazy languor

comment

eye to eye
step by step
I approach a seagull

too close!

his comment?

a blob of whiteness
    and he wings away

the Umqua

round
the round
green hills
of Oregon
swirling brown
in chocolate waves
the Upper Umqua

slipsliding
in slates
of muted jade
the Lower Umqua

tingling toes

scent of salt
    and seaweed
near-far cry of birds

seas
    grey calm
tinting rose and gold
in dawn's luminescence

swish swash
of tiny breaking waves
crunch of sand
tingling toes

backwash

in the backwash
of ebbing waters
tangle of seaweed
      and seashells
timbers weathered white
glint of broken crab legs
orange
amongst pebbles
of granite
marble and old green glass

tides

tides pull
tides push
and in sun and salt
and sand
logs
white bleached
roll on rounded rocks

no competition

in silent competition
with loons
in swift
      underwater flight

with seagulls
    diving
        effortlessly

with harbour seals
    white bellies up
        slipping smoothly
through fish-rich waters

a noisy splashing!

scuba divers
awkwardly surfacing

fall

myriad
reds and golds and amber

scents of cinnamon
nutmeg and ginger

autumn leaves
        falling

*conceiving
the pearl*

stories I tell myself

pearl

*I am a grain of sand
in the oyster of God
how do I conceive the pearl?*

Oneness

*let me
for a few shuddering
          moments
feel the presence of the One*

*let me see
the Maker of the stars
and the magnificence
of me*

*let me know
not in my mind
but in my heart
       and gut
Oneness and me*

the other side of memory

*a softness mists
in from the winter sea
a slow peace
bathes my spirit
gentles my mind
and fills the emptiness
within my hollow heart*

*and my gaze shifts
to the world out there
on the other side of memory*

powerless

*in the dusk
on the sidewalk
shawled
face grimaced into a plea
a mother suckles her child*

*I
powerless
ashamed
pass a coin*

prattle

in the splendour
of **now**
how stale and idle
the prattle of sages
the re-tattle
of the tales
of the various sons of God?

dichotomy

within me
there's a roaring
         emptiness
     bellowing
fill me!
fill me!

and a quietness
intoning
I am filled
I **am** fulfilled

shackled

*shackled
in the
heaviness
of the past*

*drifting
in dreams
of the future*

now is nowhere!

languor

*the languor of belonging
the lassitude of loving*

*such yearning
for the effortless joy
the ease
the laziness
of lasting love*

need

*this need so deep
to share
with one I love
all that is beautiful*

*the grey dappling of alders
shadowing firs
flaming madronas
straight-draped cedars*

*the tumbling of white water
the green cool of pools
the roaring sutras
          of waterfalls*

*the seamless rhythm of wind
        weaving through trees*

*the geometry of sunlight
         shafting down*

the rising blue of woodsmoke

the one-ness that is we

*life just **is***

*on the long low shores
toward the distant
fall of the waves
I walk out to sea*

*companionlike
my long shadow walks beside me
    such fine company*

*I stop
sit awhile
take in the sun
count the pebbles
measure the sea
calm now in indigo*

sudden squall!

*seahorses
    buck white
and trees respond
    soughing*

*back in the forest
soft path underfoot
and the smell of green
I greet each
age-old tree
wishing it
longevity*

continues..........

*and deeper in the depths
of green
shiverings of sunlight
dapple through the leaves
scintillating gold
in the breeze*

*walking in the forest
beside the ocean
talking
with God
life just
is
and I could die here
fulfilled*

starstuff

*although I wear vanity
like a poppinjay
it becomes me not*

*of tougher stuff
am I made
of sea
and rock
and mountain*

and of stars

hard at work

as the sun arcs
    from noon to dusk
I work hard
   throwing pebbles
      into the sea

a gull keeps me company
strutting the beach
          upwind
taking flight
   then gliding downwind
back again

just as busy as me!

resurrection

I waken
from the heavy darkness
of a deep sleep
my lips
sweet bitter dry
slaking insatiably
on the joy

on the pain of life

again!

yearning

boats anchored
riding at ease
mirrored bright
silent
in their reflections

my heart
    unrestrained
scattering
       in a thousand directions
seeking
    searching
        yearning

flowing with God

*as a log drifts
on the unseen tide
so do I
in the flow of God*

> *a pity
> this were not just
> a pretty play
> of words*

*would it were wrenched
from my heart and gut
that I could
scream to the stars*

*take me now!
let me flow with God*

on having no head

*on my canvas roof
I listen to the
tintinnabulation
of the rain*

*to the cry
of a distant gull
to the soughing
of the rising wind*

*warm in goose down
I lie about
counting the joys
of doing nothing*

*four quatrains
while lying abed
it's oh ! so simple
not using my head*

to walk again

*a wastrel life
have I led
often too blind
to the shining
of God's light
in the birds
the beaches
and the seas*

*and
particularly
in me*

*I need again
to walk a beach
of scattered seashells
bleached white and clean
by wind and salt and sea
to fly
once more
with birds
in aimless delight
filled full
with the purpose of life
and dream
sweet dreams
in deep sleep
of awakening
to find my world renewed*

alchemy

*from a footprint
in the sand
I conjured
a living
loving being*

*in this alchemy
of the mind
she reached in
and touched
my aching heart
and I was
instantly in love
and alive again
with the joy of living*

leftovers

*beaches
littered
with shells
    and feathers
and broken
    crab claws
leftovers
on these
    killing shores*

death wish

not wearing a seatbelt
nor telling anyone
*   where I was going*
I drove a hundred miles
along a far shore
then hiked another twenty
and not once
in all that while
did I a single soul encounter
nor bear
nor cougar
wolf or marmoset
nor elk
or even beaver
just trees and clouds
and mountains
and their reflections
and the warm dark wet earth
the soft sounds
of wind-ruffling water
and the softer sound
of silence

and as I hiked lost trails
I was inviting
the final coup d'grace
not from bear
or random rockfall
but from the sudden surge
that is death

continues.........

the clot of blood
the sudden loss of breath
and a body in the wilderness

but happily the sun came out
and I flung a boot
at my melancholy
and smiled
and smiled
at the absurdity of a body found
amidst my pear parings
sandwich wrappings
and sundry unfinished verse

companionship

*the mists
looming
steep
over the sea
greying the blues
cooling the sun*

*my footprints
printing
on the white sands
my soft shadow
my loving companion*

read all about it!

*I never mourned a tree
until I smelled
at Nootka Sound
a pulp mill*

*there
where mountain ranges
tumble down
so greenly
to the sea
I saw steam
pale the sky
and cadavers
in overwidth trucks
tumbrelling in
for the carnage
trucks bulging
not with commercial fir
but with ancient chained giants
ready for the claws and blades
and pungent salts
for the making of instant pulp*

*it's in the newspapers
read all about it !*

just here

*sitting cross-legged
in the sunlight
alone on the beach
I own the world*

*in my palm
the roundness of pebbles
through my eyelids
the brightness of the sun*

*on the tideline
the percussion
of plunging waves*

*counting down
from one to nothing
time collapses
and I'm*

just here

maya

bursting into the
myriad
transparent
worlds of maya
I
a bubble
blown by the Creator

granddaughter

in awe of my vast age
I sit in the sun
watching
the leaves turn gold
remembering
it was but yesterday
when I was seven

Anastasia
eyes wide
    to the wonder of the world
she is seven

benediction

*I sit on a rock
mantras and prayers
mumbling in my head*

but only for moments

*for
before me
is the sea and the sky
and the rocks
and seagulls
seaweed and sand*

*and the waves
become my mantra
the sunlight
my prayers
and the wind
      and clouds
my benediction*

ghosts

*in the Algarve
on ancient ramparts
Crusader ghosts
and shadows
of the Moors*

thunder

*how still
the mountain lake
resounding
a silence
    that thunders
in the inner chambers
of my ear*

salting the wine

*to which strange
stranger
do I need to prove
and prove again
my right to joy?*

*around what forgotten totem
must I sacrifice
the gifts of my life?*

*who is it
that chokes the breath of my joy
who salts the wine of this moment?*

*a child
lost
abandoned
trying too hard to please
to be loved
to be good*

way out

*open veins
in a blood-warm bath
a way out
ending
the senseless task
of making sense
of a non sense life*

      a way
           out *of non sense*

*sitting in the sun
watching
winter pansies grow*

a finger pointing

my spirit
a torn nail caught in silk
chalk screeched on blackboard
a brakeless car
       on a slippery road

yet

as I look into
the velvet depths of a petunia
I see
veiled in the folds

a finger pointing
at the moon

shapeshifting

god like
I soar
wide-eyed
in the blue-white sky

dream
in the green deeps of trees

drift
in the swift grey waters

quantum view

*a unique
viewpoint
am I
an
observer
fact sifting
in my
particular
singularity
knowing
what I see
is not what I see*

like stars

*trembling
shimmering
semblances
ghosts of long-lost
brightnesses
lost in light years
of silence*

like solid objects

*doppelgangers
of dancing
fields of energy*

continues..........

like loves and hatreds

*distillations merely
of my particular
chimerical chemistry*

and Truths

*inconsistent constructs
in the geometry
of change
shapeshifting
in the fields of relativity*

domino days

*from the dim loom
of the future
    the beyond beckons
and days
dominoes of death
      omens of fear
fall back upon me
  one
    upon
      the
        other*

a pocketful of poems

cliff climb
fall onto beach

aching bones

my body
on the warm sands

a fine place to die!

and as I lie on my back
I listen to the waves
breaking into my silence
washing away the beach
    washing away my years

and I have a droll thought
though macabre
my body
washed up
    on the shore
the only I D
a pocketful
    of poems

listening

lying on a rock
on an endless beach
listening
        listening

my rock sinks
    in the rising tide
waves wash my feet
I

  heedless

    listen on

bahamas

you and me
sleepy
under de lazy
tree

conchy joe
businessmon
always
on
de telephon

secret lodestone

*here am I
day upon day
life after life
sipping
endlessly
of the nectar of being
    my thirst unslaked
a secret lodestone
swinging my compass
pointing me hither
then thither*

koan

*thunderclap
splitting
creation*

*sound
of
one
hand
clapping*

outbreath

*the
endless
creation
of
galaxies*

*fireworks
of
the
outbreathing
Brahma*

right action

*picking up plastic garbage
on a pristine shore
sticky candywrappers
on forest footpaths*

*such joy
      in right action*

old movies

looping
    endlessly
through
the
sprocket
holes
of
my
mind
    old
        movies

show
me
now

please!

frames

one
  by
    one

click click click!

that are

  now

    now

      now!

dance of love

*in the dance of love
the scorpion and the butterfly
waltz
    eternally entwined
shapeshifting
    one into the other*

calm

*in the ceaseless surge
of the sea
    in the curve
of waves
endlessly breaking
how calm my soul*

at
odds
with
God

separation

This is the poetry of separation from God - the poetry of despair.

*What a fine place this separation turned out to be. Having reached bottom so many times there was only one way for me to go. Up! A new beginning - the realization that I can only know what is, by what is not. Without down I cannot know up. Without separation from God there cannot be unity with God. There cannnot be **at-one-ment**.*

*At-one-ment is the content of the next and final section of my poetry, " **as God and I awaken** ".*

at odds with God

at odds
with God's law of creation
of
predation
piled upon predation
just another denizen
in his vast killing fields
I scream
oh God of Love !
is there no other way?

and each night
in the opiate of sleep
I dream
of wakening
      into a sweeter world

eyes wet on the inside

I am a fire
burning without heat
growing old
dread in my bones

I am a fallen tree
in a dying forest
awaiting the soft
mushrooms of decay

I am a pool of tears
that will not flow
eyes wet
but on the inside

casino

spinning
on life's wheel
      powerless

it's God's casino

silence of the angels

in all this world
I have no peer
the only friend I have
is me

yet

there are angels
it is said
who love and guide

but why so silently?

heritage

my spirit departs
leaving
only bones
and the detritus
of unfond memories

grasping for the stars

fear

like nitrogen
in my bloodstream
rises
as my hand grasps
*   for the stars*
but my body
*   hangs heavy*
*   with mortality*

and in my empty heart
there is no joy
even in the awakening sky

yet
my flowers grow
and the horizon
is a sudden wash of light

oh to be free
just you
God
and me

duet playing
in my heart's chamber

legacy

my heart tightens
I ponder my legacy

a handful of haiku

unfurled rosebud

how dark my heart?
how red the intimacies
in an unfurled rosebud?

how soon the blooming?
how soon the uncurling
of the layers of love?

swifter than a smile

*the joy that is now
is swifter than a smile
fleeter than a heartbeat*

*it waits not the morrow
nor dallies
in the mildew of memory*

*but I
distant cousin of joy
await the dawn
choke in that mildew*

quicksands

trying to dig
        my way out
with a teaspoon
I
son of eternity
sinking
in the quicksands of time

where
God
are you?
and for whom do you care
in this frightful universe?

is there no way to learn
other than pain?

where
God
is your embrace?
were You there at all?
at all?
or
did the Big Bang bang
without you?

fullness and emptiness

*my head
filled full with facts
I search the stars
for meaning*

and then I scream!

*for in my heart
at my core
there is an emptiness
that no ocean can fill full*

arch predator

*it seems
dear Lord
that your focused
    infinite attention
upon the
      tiered
      lavish destruction
of one species by the other
created
that final killing critter*

man

arch predator

beyond good and evil

*stretched
on the rack of the world
searching for God
I find
    only a void
and a creation
beyond good or evil*

oblivious

*happening
    all at its own pace*

bearer of bandages

my soul
 flinches

flenced

and the bleeding
 does not cease

I have incanted
with you gods of old
 muttered faithfully
your formulae

I have bowed
deeply
to Allah
sat cross-legged with
 Lords Buddha
and Krishna
 crossed myself
for Christ

found only bandaids

until

 finally

all that's left is me
 bearer of my own bandages

I wonder

dear God
I look at your mountains
and trees
and your abundant bounty
and I see
too
all the pain in your creation

and I wonder

                      and I wonder

and as I drink my wine
I ponder
the nostrums
of spiritual cant
and the mystery
of the here
                      and anywhere
of the quantum boys

so sad
to be so finite
when
dear God
everything's
      just
            not
that

last gasp

in each
    vanishing moment
a crumb is a feast
a breath
all there is

embracing
that last gasp
I implode
into
the
Black
Hole
that
is
God

futureless

in the husk of the year
I sit
futureless
grinding out
    old dreams

a sigh for stanley

in the forest silence
alone beneath the trees
and the fall of rain
    and maple leaves
I tread a path
    of beaten gold

on the trail
around each bend
water falls
in white waterfalls
and the air is misted
sweet
and cool

on dripping logs
I cross a stream
    pause
breathe deeply

and sigh
a sigh
for stanley
watch
his tears
    drown
        in the flowing waters

empty

*running on empty
holding
    my last breath
beyond my last prayer*

out of sync

*grubbing
for
meaning
eyes closed
ears plugged
nostrils stopped
heart
one beat
out of sync
with God's*

the why?

of the
how
I sort of know
also of the
where

but what of the
why?

have I survived
to die
in such bewilderment?

where am I?

when I open my hand
where is my fist?
when I die
where am I ?

as God and I awaken
at-one-ment

*After being **"at Odds with God"** in the previous section of my poetry when I was separate from God and in the deeps of despair - I could only go up. Thus I came to know God by what God is not! Without knowing down I could not know up. And that's how I awakened and, from time to time, came to places of at-one-ment - the content of this section.*

as God and I awaken

between Thee
          and me
a mutual re-cognition

a first step

a re-awakening

a re-membrance
of our heritage divine
as Thee and I
yawn
and awake from our sleep
in the material worlds
where together
we
fell
lost for aeons
in our senses
our heritage
remembered
only in dreams
of the starbursts
      of our birth
when starseeds
were scattered
      out into the worlds
to grow new galaxies
        to grow new gods

behind the dream

*I feel it
as flowers do
as birds flying
trees growing*

*I know it
behind the dream
beyond the heart*

*that Oneness
that is me*

starmaker

*I am a starchild
one with the Starmaker
and no thing
       is not me*

the message

*I closed my eyes
and asked God
to show himself*

*open your eyes
He said*

apprentice

*a wild carpenter
is the devil
hacking out his
jigsaw pieces*

*God's apprentice
am I
assembling
the bits
solving the puzzle*

eating my soup

*lacking nutrition
each hungry day
bellies out into the next
and my neediness
re-echoes the emptiness
in my heart*

what to do?

*I will not
diminish the sunlight
by being shaded
by another*

I've learned the lesson

*in this life
to enliven life
there's just me*

I listen within

*God says
be beholden to no man
or woman
be beholden
not even to Me
but to the spirit
that is thee*

*so I eat my soup
watch my flowers grow
and attend
    to the next moment*

there!

in the bumble of bees
in the cry of a gull
there
there
speaks my Lord

in the caress of the breeze
in the warmth of the sun
there
there
is His touch

in shining pebbles
tumbling in the waves
there
there
moves my Lord

in a seagull soaring
in an engine revving
there
there
lies the glory of the Lord

in each cell

   in my every breath
there
   there!
beats the heart of God

God filled full

*embedded
in the granite of ages
I remain
a gem of God
ready to implode
replete with experience
to fill full my God*

thunder

*among myriad sounds
and the chaos
    of thoughts
the silence
of God
thunders*

remembrance

*bemused
in the
quick-cut
    tv
       world
of senses
my span of attention
collapses
into
bytes
of
  this
    and
that*

*but
lost in the myriad
demands
of needs
and wants
my fallen spirit
remembers
      from time
   to time
my stellar heritage
my One-ness with God*

wonder

my final journey

*the wonder of me
becoming the wonder of We*

co-creators

*it is I
through whom
God manifests
it is I
who create
    the worlds*

experiencing

*God's apprentice
am I
experiencing all*

whisper

*a whisper of grass
bending in the wind*

God in small things

that's me

all
nothing
and
both

that's
me

now

*this
moment*

*all
I'll
ever
own*

God tallies

*on this world
        my imprint
a brief footprint
in the sand
washed away by the tide*

*but
among galaxies
countless to man
God tallies the grains*

a fine place to die

*in my room
sunlight on the walls
luminous
like the inner chambers
of a shell*

*outside my window
in the dome of a cobalt sky
birds
frolicking
    to and fro
in the warm winter sunshine*

*in my bed
propped on my pillows
my cat on my lap
I talk with God*

*He agrees
this could be a fine place to die*

beginnings

I spoke
with God
my new-found friend
"is it time to go?"
I asked
"your work has just begun."

the stream

neither
flotsam
nor
jetsam

the stream
am
I

dormant starseed

*twixt here and nowhere
in the now and ever
I
the silent witness*

*I
dormant
who
from the volcanic depths
of my heart
create the worlds*

what more?

to hear
the great green ocean
sigh
as it moves
rolling from tide to tide

to walk
a beach
crunch the sand
watch
    my shadow
        striding beside me

to name
birds by their plumage
clouds
by their patterns of white

what more?

to watch
gulls in flight
and rocks standing
        solitary

what more than this?

growling into gear

to sit in the early morning sunlight
and watch
the blossoms unfolding

to see
the mists lifting
and the silhouettes of trees and hills
etching black

to scan
the distant sea
and hear
the ceaseless surge of waves

to feel the breeze gentling my skin
   in long
      good morning caresses

feel the tears behind my eyes
as the day's cares shudder into shape

and then to remember
when the sun is shining
and the birds are calling
God is abounding
and how easy it is
to forget the glory
when the day growls into gear

juggler

*so easy to surmise
that the muted
tumbling of the galaxies
are not
the juggling hand of God
but that of some other
cosmic clown*

*easier to know
that in each single
act of kindness
there
there!
is the hand of God*

emptiness fullness

inside my silence
a supernova
exploding
into
 God
    transcendent

in my heart
His heartbeat
in my breath
His inbreathing
  and outbreathing
as galaxies flower and wither
as energy ceaselessly changes
  from fullness
     to emptiness
    emptiness
     to fullness

there am I

*in the thud
of waves against rock
in the squelch
of sneakers
in mud-soaked grass
in the flow
of raindrops
down my cheeks
in the ingoing
and outgoing
of my breath*

    there am I

mindful

in the moment

I am the stream

*I am
towering
in the glory of trees
dreaming
green dreams
in the long lines
       of lovely pines
I am
falling
dappling
rippling
through the leaves
leaves
heavy with sunlight
down
down
to the stream*

*I am the stream
alone
and cloned with All That Is*

I am

dimension of love

scissored into time
cut
into the dimension
                    of fear
my soul cries

then remembers home
in the timeless dimension of love
where God and I are One

*I am **that** I am*

*a quantum blur
of energy
and information
am
I*

*here
    there
everywhere
    and nowhere*

*a point
no point*

*a possibility
in all possibilities*

*I am **that** I am*

at-one-ment

my love
enfolds the world
envelops the galaxies
melts into God

I am
the
shining
dewdrop
slipping
into the shining sea
as the sea
slips
into
me

ISBN 1552124231
9 781552 124239